CREEPY BUT COOL DINOSAURS

Alan Walker

A Crabtree Seedlings Book

CRABTREE
Publishing Company
www.crabtreebooks.com

TABLE OF CONTENTS

A WORLD OF DINOSAURS

The first dinosaurs roamed Earth over 240 million years ago.

Plateosaurus lived in the Triassic period.

Some dinosaurs were as tall as five-story buildings. Others were the size of small birds.

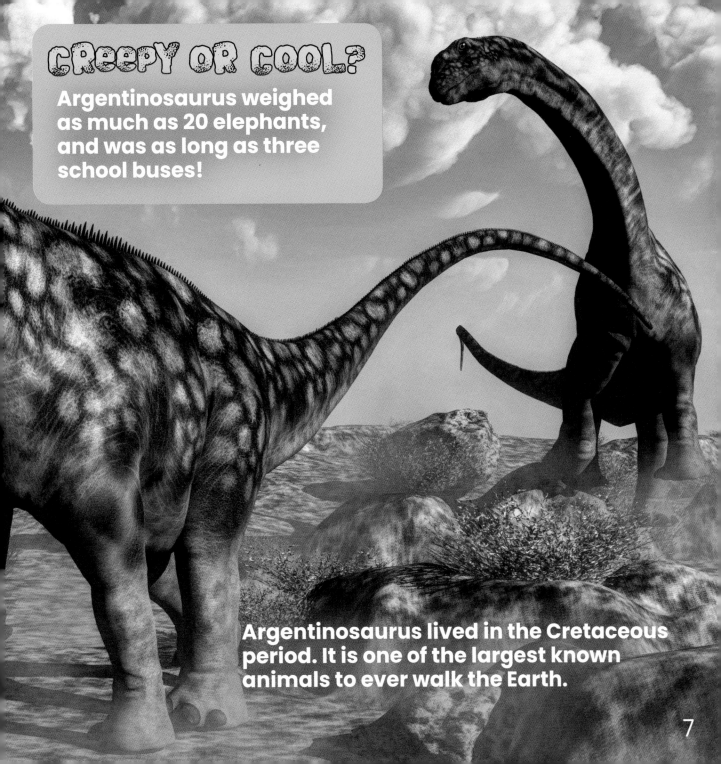

Argentinosaurus weighed as much as 20 elephants, and was as long as three school buses!

Argentinosaurus lived in the Cretaceous period. It is one of the largest known animals to ever walk the Earth.

Dinosaurs lived all over the world.

CREEPY OR COOL?
The word *dinosaur* means terrible lizard.

DID YOU KNOW?
Humans never lived on Earth at the same time as dinosaurs.

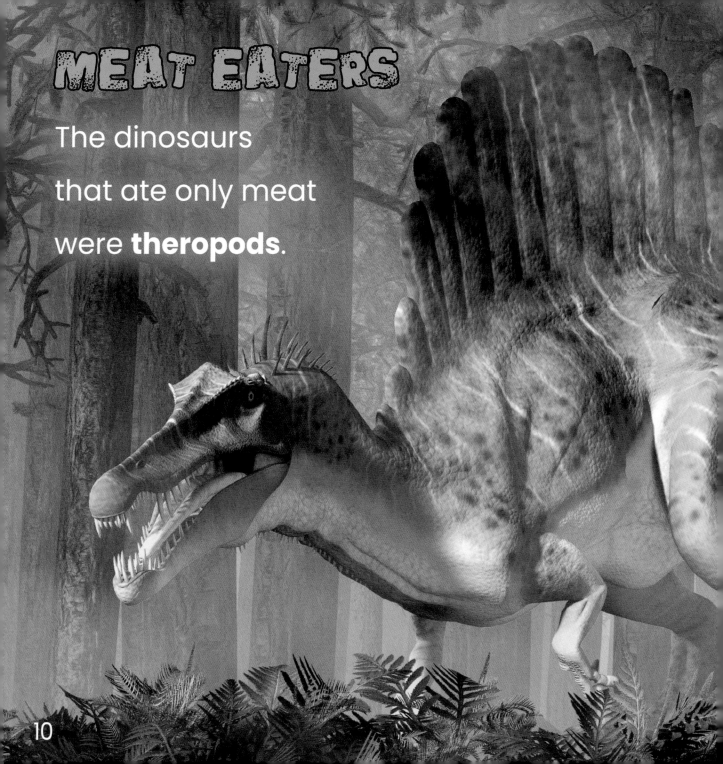

MEAT EATERS

The dinosaurs
that ate only meat
were **theropods**.

Spinosaurus was the biggest of all meat-eating dinosaurs. Scientists believe it ate mostly fish.

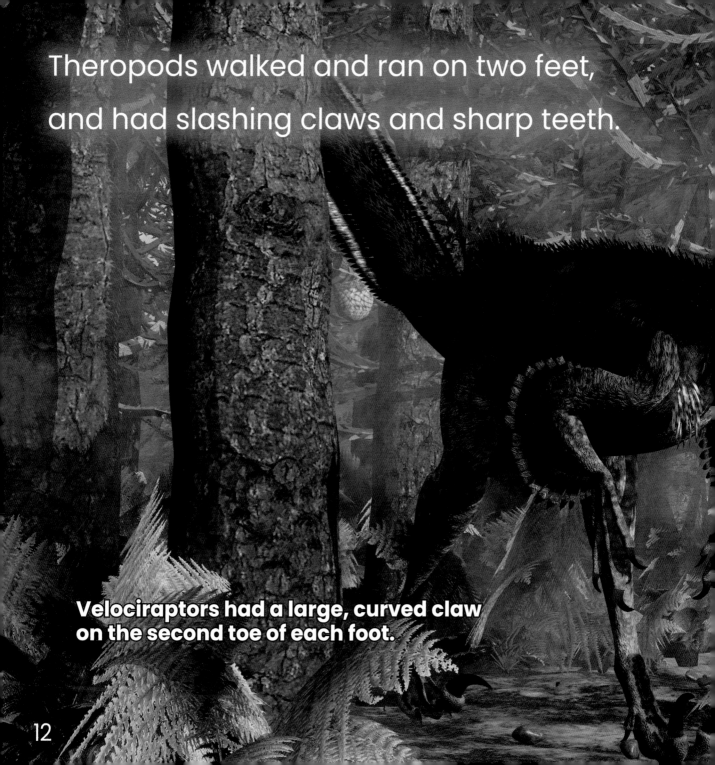

Theropods walked and ran on two feet, and had slashing claws and sharp teeth.

Velociraptors had a large, curved claw on the second toe of each foot.

CREEPY OR COOL?

Scientists believe Velociraptors had feathers—for warmth not flying. They also believe that birds are the closest living relatives of dinosaurs today.

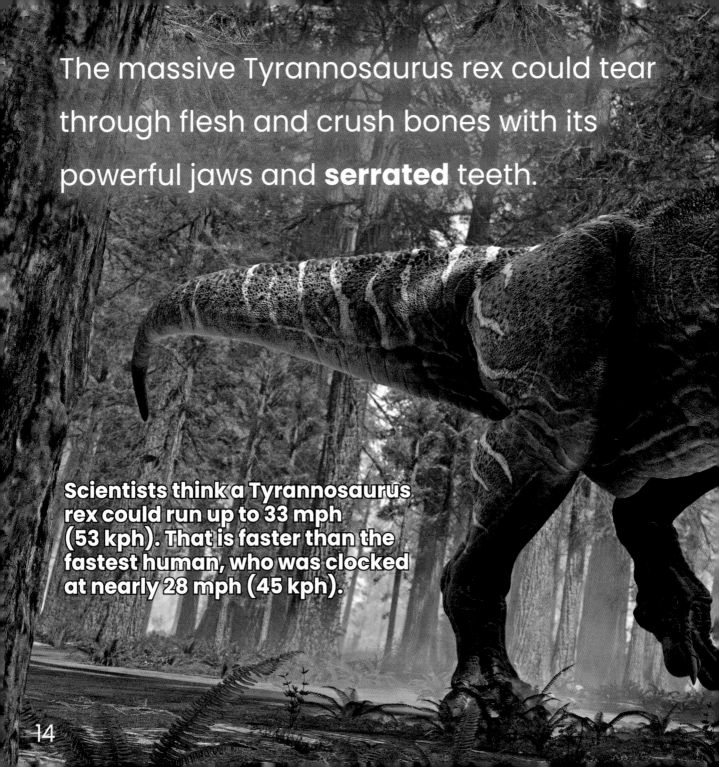

The massive Tyrannosaurus rex could tear through flesh and crush bones with its powerful jaws and **serrated** teeth.

Scientists think a Tyrannosaurus rex could run up to 33 mph (53 kph). That is faster than the fastest human, who was clocked at nearly 28 mph (45 kph).

CREEPY OR COOL?

Fossils show that the T. rex had a 5-foot- (one-and-a-half-meter-) long skull. And yes, you could easily fit in its mouth!

PLANT EATERS

The dinosaurs that ate only plants were often **prey** for the meat eaters. Many plant-eating dinosaurs moved in groups to stay safe.

Brachiosaurus was a sauropod.

Triceratops used its large horns to protect itself from **predators**.

CReePY OR COOL?

Triceratops means three-horned face.

Ankylosaurus was a large **herbivore**—about three times as long as your bed!

CREEPY OR COOL?

Ankylosaurus had bony plates growing out of its skin. These could protect it like armor.

DINOSAUR DETECTIVES

Paleontologists are like dinosaur detectives. They study the clues left behind by fossils.

Fossil Clues:

Bones give clues about the size of a dinosaur.

Footprints can tell us if the dinosaur walked on four feet, or two.

Teeth can tell us if the dinosaur was a plant eater or a meat eater.

Poop fossils give clues about what dinosaurs ate!

We don't know why dinosaurs went **extinct** 65 million years ago. But we do know many more of their fossils are yet to be found.

Stegosaurus fossil

dinosaur eggs fossil